WHEN YOU CAN'T GO HOME

PORTRAITS OF REFUGEES IN THE PACIFIC NORTHWEST

To all my new friends featured in this book,
for opening your hearts and homes to us.

CONTENTS

INTRODUCTION

These stories break hearts, and that's a good thing.

We're facing the world's biggest refugee crisis since World War II. When my eyes first opened to the level of horror and abject discouragement faced by these men, women, and children, I spent an embarrassing amount of time despairing and journaling. Then, at last, my sweet husband asked, "So what are you going to do about it?"

I realized then that though I claimed to be for refugees, I didn't know any. Thus began my journey to do what I do best: change issues into stories, and associate those stories with faces. Ten refugees in the Pacific Northwest have bravely offered up their stories. They agreed to be painted and interviewed about the most harrowing period of their lives and how they have overcome, so that we may listen and learn from their experiences. For every book you purchase—for yourself, for a friend, for a community—50% of the proceeds go directly to World Relief, an organization helping these refugees work through the chaos of escaping danger and settling into their new homes.

I am just a painter, you are just a reader. But it takes all of us to stand against injustice. We can fight the temptation of apathy through humanizing our global neighbors, and through engaging in practical advocacy, many methods of which are listed at the back of this book.

It starts today, a partnership between you, me, and those who need their voices to be heard. Because even though shattered hearts are better than apathy, it's not enough to be broken by what we see. We must also aspire to be part of the solution.

Karisa Keasey

MERHAWI HABTEAB

ERITREA

"I was going to be in boat when it sink."

That's how Merhawi would describe this day years later. He and his new bride, Ziad, clung to each other. Ziad's tears mingled with the rain, and her cries rose with the water around her waist. They were in the middle of the Mediterranean Sea in the dead of night, packed in a rickety old boat with 70 other refugees – a boat made for 30. Out of options, they had fled war-torn Libya with only the breath in their lungs and the clothes on their backs.

Halfway to where asylum waited on the shores of Malta, Italy, the boat began to sink. They had narrowly escaped one death, only to be caught in the clutches of another. "We had one life jacket," explained Merhawi. "Ziad lost hers. I don't know, I think someone took it from her. I gave her mine. I know how to swim. I don't want to see her die." Their dreams of growing old together were dashed in the waves. Merhawi's lifelong desire to become a doctor flashed before his eyes, and he believed it would never come to fruition.

When Merhawi was a child, you could hear his pattering feet trailing his father as the man distributed medications, refreshed bandages, and cleaned out wounds. Though Merhawi's father was not an educated doctor, he did what he could to fulfill the desperate need for medical care in his community. Eritrea was in an ongoing war with Ethiopia for independence, leaving its citizens desolate.

One morning, Merhawi was awakened by the slamming of doors and rustling of feet. "I remember there was a bus accident," recalled Merhawi. His father had come bursting in the door of their small home, supporting the weight of a woman named Sarah. She had suffered a broken arm in the accident. Despite his mother's protests to take her to the hospital, Merhawi's father was determined to intervene.

"In Eritrea, they were quick to cut off limbs if they are broken, instead of trying to fix it," Merhawi explained. Resolved to save the arm, Merhawi's father took Sarah under their own roof and nurtured her back to health. With pride, Merhawi recalls his father's unwavering determination. "He helped a lot of people in the community – they respected him. I want to go to school and be a doctor so I can help people."

But in Eritrea, his chances of being able to pursue a career in medicine were

"

I was going to be in boat when it sink.

"

slim. Living in Eritrea meant that the government dictated almost every aspect of one's life. This included one's career choice. "You can't choose whatever you want. If I wanted to go to be a doctor, I can't go. It's not our choice."

Every citizen at the age of 16 is forced to attend military school where methods of torture, humiliation, rape, and forced labor have been used as a way to coerce cooperation. One method of torture Eritrean exiles have referred to is called "the eight." Hoisted in the air upside-down with hands and ankles tied behind them, the soles of the victim's feet are shredded with a whip. They are left this way for days on end. The excruciating pain and position render their limbs paralyzed for weeks, often leaving permanent damage. They have been known to use these sadistic torture methods on the family of conscripts who refused to serve or deserted. Merhawi recalls barely surviving his first year, "You have to go and do whatever they want, like how to shoot...I went one year and it was so hard, I can't handle it. So, then we escaped to Sudan."

In Sudan, Merhawi met his wife Ziad at a school at which they both taught. Struck by her character and beauty, he

soon married her. The ceremony was bittersweet. They knew it would be the last time they would see their families for a long time, if not forever. Together they crossed the border of Sudan to Libya in order to further their distance from Eritrea. Living in a primarily Muslim culture as Christians, however, held its own set of difficulties.

"One of the hardest parts... you have to be clothed like Muslim. Ziad had to wear her Hijab. They don't allow us to be together. Woman is separate and man is separate. (Gesturing to Ziad) This is my wife. But they don't care." On top of the cultural complications, war broke out in 2011. "It was insane. Everybody had guns and would be drunk, shooting off." Afraid for their lives, Merhawi and Ziad disembarked from the shores of Libya at 2:00 am on a harrowing journey across the Mediterranean Sea, in hopes of seeking asylum in Malta, Italy.

The old engine heaved its last sputtering breath, leaving the lethal ocean waves to claim them. In a last desperate attempt, the captain made a futile call for help over the radio. Even if someone were to hear them, they knew the probability of someone harvesting them for their organs, selling them to slavery, or returning them to Eritrea was high. In resignation, Ziad took Merhawi's hand, drawing him towards her.

"Come, let's be together the minutes that we have," her voice rasped, spent from the cries that were swallowed by the dark. Merhawi kissed the crown of her head, and they uttered prayers under their breath.

Suddenly, a crackling voice was heard on the radio, breaking the silence. The voice, claiming to be with the Red Cross, was asking for their location. The approaching boat was met first with skepticism, then relief when they found it was indeed the Red Cross. "We really didn't believe our eyes," Merhawi remembered thinking, "Is it true? These people really come to save us?"

As they were handed dry clothes and warm blankets, reality began to sink in. They were alive, and it looked like they would stay that way.

Merhawi and Ziad were fortunate in their rescue. Thousands of Eritrean refugees die each year fleeing war and persecution, either from starvation and dehydration in the Sahara Desert or by drowning in the Mediterranean Sea. Of the 11,564 Eritrean refugees that arrived on the shores of Italy in 2015, at least 2,692 were found dead.

With the rest of their lives ahead of them, Merhawi and Ziad made plans for their next steps to freedom. They applied for refugee status through the UNHCR in 2012. While they waited to hear back, Merhawi began going to school to pursue his dream of becoming a doctor. While Malta had provided an immediate solution to their plight, they knew it was not their forever home. Not being allowed citizenship meant that they could be sent back to Eritrea at any moment.

After the birth of their son Naod, the need to find a permanent home became more pressing. Finally, after five years of hard work and waiting, Merhawi's family was granted refugee status and they embarked on a seventeen-hour ride to America.

Nestled safely in their apartment in Kent, Washington, Ziad performs the Eritrean coffee ceremony from her homeland, with little Naod nursing at her chest. Coffee fumes waft around the room.

"

We really didn't believe our eyes. Is it true? These people really come to save us?

"

"I want to do everything for my son and for his education," said Merhawi, his voice wrought with emotion as he regards his wife and child lovingly from across the room.

Merhawi is now a certified phlebotomist and looking forward to continuing his education to further help people as a doctor.

Someday, Naod will go to preschool, and a teacher will ask, "What do you want to be when you grow up?" And Naod will answer with whatever his little heart desires: a privilege for which Merhawi and Ziad crossed land and sea.

"Merhawi and Naod"
16"x20" Watercolor

"Ziad and Naod"
16"x20" Watercolor

"Ziad and Naod in the Kitchen"
16"x20" Watercolor

TAGHREED EL-SHEIKH

IRAQ

"

I miss my lovely city Baghdad, because we used to live there
together, with family, my kids, and friends.

"

Taghreed dishes out homemade klaicha to her guests in Seattle. She's a parade of smiles and bangles in her traditional Jellabiya attire. "I miss my lovely city, Baghdad," she says, "because we used to live there together, with family, my kids, and friends." She recalls blissful days dancing in the kitchen with her mother-in-law, learning the family recipes.

Taghreed's passion for food won her the top prize from a famous Turkish cooking competition, which took place while she and her family were residing as refugees in Istanbul. "I love cooking, because I believe food brings people together. Sharing food means love, because food is love."

Prior to the 2003 war in Iraq, Taghreed's meals were well-known for uniting people in her neighborhood which was comprised of individuals from a variety of backgrounds. Her eyes light up as she recalls a pre-war Baghdad, where many guests of Christian, Yezidi, Mandae'i, Muslim and Jewish backgrounds all gathered around one table as neighbors, friends, and colleagues.

Despite Taghreed's outward ebullience, there are shards of pain, a vestige of the memories of her home. Bending over a well-worn photo album of her daughter's wedding, she recounted those happy days with her family before they were confronted by war. "April 9, the day Baghdad was invaded, is the worst day in my life," Taghreed's son, Mohamed, remembers, "because, this is when we woke up watching the American forces filling the streets of the Capital." Threatened by Iran backed militia and suspicious of the United States occupiers, Taghreed and her family left Baghdad for the first time. "Fearing for our Sunni identity, we said goodbye to Baghdad, and she said, 'See you later,'" Taghreed lamented.

After escaping Iraq, Taghreed lived in several countries before applying for refuge in Turkey with the United Nations in 2010. By 2013, she and her husband, along with their teenage son, were placed in Seattle, where World Relief met them. Like many refugees, the largest source of devastation was the emotional turmoil of being uprooted from her home and family. "At the beginning, when we arrived, I was just crying...just being far away from my country, my kids, and my job as an accountant... I want all of us to reunite and live together like it was in Iraq," Taghreed grieves. World Relief walked with Taghreed through this process and are now working on obtaining refugee status for the rest of her adult children so they can all be reunited in America. "My kids are all my life. If one day my dream [to be with all her children again] comes true, I'm going to be the happiest mom in the world... I have hope now," she says with a smile. "All people at World Relief are like family."

Taghreed's youngest son, Mohamed, is now a University of Washington graduate with a bachelor of arts in Political Science and Jewish Studies. Before he starts graduate school, he is interning with a global American-Israeli advocacy group and an Arab-European institute on a research project in Jerusalem. Like his mother, Mohamed has a heart for breaking down barriers between people groups caused by religious extremism.

Taghreed continues to create community through her passion for cooking by working with Project Feast, an organization that supports refugees. At Project Feast, Taghreed worked hard to earn a position giving lectures about Iraqi cuisine. She combines cultural and historical components of Iraq's rich diversity with its multi-ethnic dishes, to tell the story of a people and their land.

In and out of the classroom, Taghreed loves being able to share her knowledge, skill, and vibrant personality with her students. Through food and entertainment, she creates a space for people to ask questions, share, and have community. "I am happy when people ask me about my religion and my culture. Their listening to me means a lot for me. I am so thankful for those who are thankful and appreciative."

Taghreed is helping ease the emotional pain of other refugees like herself, one kleicha at a time.

"Taghreed"
16"x20" Watercolor

"Iraqi Tea"
14"x14" Watercolor

"Kleicha"
14"x14" Watercolor

MYKHAILO KUZOMKA

UKRAINE

It was the third dead animal this month.

Until that moment, a routine morning had passed in Mykhailo's home that he had built with his family and friends. He settled for nothing but perfection for his wife Nadia, his sons Mark and Mykhailo Jr., and daughter Aviheia. Home was both their fortress and their place of worship.

He hummed a hymn as he shuffled into his coat. He reached for the front door, groaning as it pivoted. His family was still asleep, tucked safely within the sanctuary he designed. Frowning a little, he leaned down and ran his hand along the noise-making culprit. A couple of screws were loose in one of the hinges. He resolved to fix it later, and then sighed and closed the door behind him, trapping the heat inside. He breathed in deeply, letting the frigid air fill his lungs. He walked the short pathway from his home to the small church on their property, where he would set up for worship practice.

Then he saw it: the decapitated body of a large stork, lying in the grass.

"They threw them in our yard – dead animals to attack our family spiritually and mentally. We don't know who it is," he would later recall.

A chill radiated through his body as he gazed on the mutilated body. Did they wish such violence on his children, here in their own home? Was it not enough that he was discriminated against in the workplace? Breaking from his trance, he fetched a shovel from the side of the house, flexed the cold from his stiff hands, and shoveled away the gruesome carcass.

His little ones might be despised (as their parents before), but he could protect them, at least, from seeing this.

Mykhailo and his family were Protestants in a community hostile to such faith. They were beginning to buckle under the stress and worry about their children's future. How many more days would he have to see his children come home hurting?

"They were called Shtunda," he recalls much later, "a discriminatory word used for Protestants."

Mykhailo and his wife Nadia were thankful that Christians no longer paid a penalty for practicing their religion, as Nadia's parents and grandparents did under the Soviet Union. However, new fear blossoms at the growth of the Russian Orthodox Church, barreling in from the East. The Russian Orthodox Church considered Protestants an abomination.

"

They threw them in our yard   dead animals to attack our family spiritually and mentally.

"

"Russian Orthodox tries to be as a state religion in Ukraine," Mykhailo explains, adding grimly, "In future, it may be problem for non-Orthodox." The residue of atheism left by the Soviet Union and the spreading influence of the Russian Orthodox Church trapped Mykhailo's family in a crossfire of intolerance.

Additional tensions were mounting in Ukraine. The economy continued to plummet as a result of an ongoing war between Russian separatists, backed by the Russian military. Ukraine fought for land that Russia conquered in 2014. Though the fighting was mainly in the East, the war radiated out, shaking the whole country, resulting in over 10,000 civilian deaths from 2014 to 2018. Mykhailo solemnly recalled the state of his beloved country, "We lose our economy. Now, a lot of people are low income. They don't have opportunities to live. They are in the surviving process. We have a lot of problems with corruption. In daily life, people who try to be in the gospel, in religion, are harmed from others...In that period, we did not understand who will help us. We did not understand at that time what we should do."

Out of options, Mykhailo and Nadia took the brave and exhausting step of applying for refugee status. Things seemed to be going smoothly between the health screenings, interviews, and paperwork.

Then the phone rang. It was Mykhailo's boss, telling him to come in.

Somehow, his employers had heard about Mykhailo's request for refugee status and did not approve. They began looking for a way to replace him. This was the second time Mykhailo had lost his job due to religious or political bias. Mykhailo recalled the first incident. "My regional manager asked me, 'What can you tell me about your religion.' I told him... and I lost my job." Mykhailo found other means of supporting his family, every day checking the mail to see if their plea for relocation had been heard.

Three years later, the letter finally came, explaining that their family was granted refugee status. Even then, more obstacles stood in the way of his family's exodus, including a brief travel ban that extended their stay. Relief and reality hit all at once as they said goodbye to family and friends, and packed up what belongings they could.

Mykhailo's daughter Aviheia, age 10, pushed her strands of long hair out of her face as she sifted through the numerous drawings that had kept her company through long winter days. Her fingers found the corner of her favorite one, and she took a moment to savor it. She brimmed with pride whenever she thought of her father's craftsmanship, and so she had sketched herself looking over the windowsill of her childhood home. In the window, she had drawn the breathtaking expanse of her homeland. Buildings like castles dot the landscape, the real-life setting of a fairy tale. The house her father built had been its own castle to her, a stronghold she must now leave behind. Tenderly, she packed the paper away with her belongings, wondering if America had fairy tales too.

In her room in Kent, Washington, Aviheia sits, drawing at her easel. Sunshine pours through the window, alighting on her blonde crown of hair. She hums softly along with the song her tato (dad) sings from the living room. She can hear the soft "voom voom" of her four-year-old brother, Mark, playing with his toy cars. Dishes clink in the kitchen as her momma clears away the borscht they had for lunch, its aroma lingering in their apartment like a welcome friend.

Mykhailo beckons his family to come play music with him. He runs his hand down the well-loved frets of his guitar as he hears his family settle at their respective instruments.

The small apartment with traffic rushing by is a far cry from their house in Ukraine, but Mykhailo is thankful. They're together, and they're safe—free to worship their God. Their life has opened to a blank page, a fresh start. Mykhailo observes, "I like the process where we can develop something... You can see the picture when something is destroyed and by hard work, we make it better. It is philosophy of my life to increase the situation around me. Physically and spiritually."

As his eyes brim with pride for his family, they begin worshipping in unison, singing, "You are my hiding place... Whenever I am afraid I will trust in You... Let the weak say I am strong in the strength of the Lord."

"

In that period, we did not understand who will help us. We did not understand at that time what we should do.

"

"View from Home in Ukraine"
by Aviheia Kuzomka

"Mykhailo and Mykhailo Jr."
16"x20" Watercolor

"Mark Playing Guitar"
16"x20" Watercolor

"Nadiia"
16"x20" Watercolor

"Aviheia Drawing"
16"x20" Watercolor

DURGA CHUWAN

BHUTAN

They sit cross-legged in the grass. The sun reflects on the dew in the community garden, highlighting Durga's contagious smile. She sits in a bright green kameez with a dupatta draped around her head, binding her midnight silk hair. Her husband, Phauda, sits beside her, twirling blades of grass. Durga's laugh lines deepen as she grins, sharing about her beloved homeland, Bhutan.

"I love to garden. Our land was big. We had animals, cows, and big garden. My parents were farmers too."

Durga repositions her ebony braid over her shoulder. Every strand is an act of rebellion: the ethnic Napali Bhutanese were stripped of the right to wear their native clothing, language, and long hair as the Bhutanese government forced cultural assimilation. Durga refused to cut her tresses. Through sunshine and hardship, she had kept it, a beacon of her Nepali heritage and her journey to freedom.

The first Nepali residents in Bhutan go back to the 1600s, when the Bhutanese brought them over to work on temples, roads, and other developments. The Nepali residents settled in the rich green south of Bhutan where the farms became the primary food source for Bhutan. In 1958, many Nepali Bhutanese were finally given citizenship and rights through the Nationality Law of Bhutan. Even though they were officially Bhutanese residents, they held onto their rich Nepali Hindu roots. As their numbers grew and leadership shifted, the Bhutanese government grew increasingly concerned, fearing that the dual culture threatened their national unity. In 1980, the government developed the "One Nation, One People" policy. Under this law, those who could not prove tax payment before 1958 had their citizenship revoked.

It was a thinly-veiled trick. Since most Nepali were not granted citizenship until 1958, they had no tax record prior to that year. This made it easy for the government to revoke their longstanding citizenship and brand them as illegal immigrants.

Phauda looks up, his voice cracking as sadness creases his brow, "Bhutan government was opposed to the southern Bhutanese. The Nepali language was banned. The clothing was banned. The culture was banned. Books were banned. The women had to cut their hair." Durga nods, subconsciously combing her fingers through the end of her braid.

Tensions rose as the Nepali people were denied education and jobs. Protests began to break out. The government responded with ransacked villages, imprisonment, torture, rape, and often death for the Nepali people. "The government was angry," laments Phauda. "They came with the army and police. We just want our culture. We had to hide. Some people go to the jail; [police] are hitting, and many people they killing."

Ethnic cleansing had begun.

35-year-old Durga walked with her husband and three children, meager packs slung across their backs as government officials threatened them off their land. As she pivoted to look back at the only home she had ever known, her foot sunk in soil that her community had routinely tilled and harvested through the years. Tears fragmented the last image she would ever see of her homestead. Wisps of hair, escaped from her rebellious braid, caught on her hand as she wiped at her tears, and she watched her home shrink into the hills.

Withered and broken, they arrived at a refugee camp, first in Beldangi and then to Khudunabari, Jhapa Nepal with their three young children. Though they were culturally Nepali, they were not given the option of obtaining citizenship in Nepal. Some held on to hope that Bhutan would let them back into their home, but that hope proved futile, replaced by malnutrition, disease, and crime.

"Every aspect of life was hard living in refugee camp. Life was very challenging. Full of difficulties," says Durga, her mouth drooping where the lines on her skin once showed a smile. A camp is where she raised her children—where she taught them to hope, to dream, to work hard, and never give up; where she saw them marry and dream of a bigger life than what they knew.

For 20 years, Durga's feet rushed to the same faucet shared by 300 people before their allotted access time was up, carrying clean water to her family. With their weary hands, Phauda and Durga patched up the home of bamboo and plastic, protecting their hut from flooding as best they could. Each person was allotted five kilograms of rice for 15 days, vegetable oil, sugar, salt and some vegetables. At night, women and children were especially vulnerable, as rape, crime and abuse were common. Substance abuse also occurred as people tried to drown their strife, entering a

> "
>
> Bhutan government was opposed to the southern Bhutanese. The Napoli language was banned. The clothing was banned. The culture was banned.
>
> "

cycle with no future. Though Durga and Phauda were able to open a small shop to support their family, the physical and emotional poverty left more than empty stomachs. By 2007, 20 years after they arrived, over 13,000 people were packed in the Khudunabari refugee camp, still wandering aimlessly in their brokenness, wrought by their cultural genocide. Over 100,000 Nepali Bhutanese had been displaced.

In 2007, the UNHCR began resettling Bhutanese refugees. Durga and her family were informed that they would be relocated to Kent, Washington, in America.

Recalling this news with a bittersweet air, she says, "It was our only option. That time was very hard. Because I could not speak the English and could not understand." Adding English to the strand of languages she already knew seemed a daunting task at her age. While she was overjoyed to find a place where her children and grandchildren could put down roots, receive health care, and work towards earning citizenship, fear gripped her at the thought of settling in a foreign country.

The bustle of the airport still rung in her ears as she followed her son through SeaTac airport with her family. Her head pounded from the overload of information being dumped on her. The shock of cold Washington air felt like knives on her skin. She held her braid to her chest, finding her familiar strands of strength. The next few days were a fog of confusion learning to adjust to running water, refrigerators, job applications and paperwork.

Some days Durga awoke with a heavy heart, invisible strings pulling her to a home thousands of miles away. She could never return. Now she utters, "I felt lost, misled. Away from my friends and relatives. Hardest part was language and navigation." Learning English and familiarizing herself with the land helped Durga feel a sense of belonging, but it was the community around her that made the greatest difference. Durga joined the community garden group through World Relief, where she was given a garden to nurture and grow. It felt good to dip her hands in the moist soil again and create life beyond her own. With a net of community around them to turn to, Durga, Phauda and their family began to sprout hope that they could make America their home. Beaming with giddy laughter, she announced, "I went to a citizen class... We all family get citizenship in 2016!" Pride radiated from her for her family and their perseverance through the trials they had gone through.

Durga's depression upon their initial resettlement is not uncommon at all. Thousands of refugees relocate each year, and though they are safe and thankful for refuge, it is not home; at least not right away. Settling into another culture is difficult enough, let alone trying to do so when you are older with little to no income, no support system, psychological symptoms from past trauma, and medical struggles from lack of proper health care over the years. An invitation for a fresh start does not always guarantee success, particularly for the elderly. Many battle with depression, shaped from decades of displacement and a loss of cultural and personal identity, mounted by physical and emotional isolation of living in a foreign land with limited mobility. Suicide has become increasingly prevalent among refugees as the number of displaced people has reached the highest number ever recorded worldwide. Depression and suicide rates are particularly high for Bhutanese refugees because of the time spent in refugee camps, and again increases dramatically for the elderly. Creating a net of community and

relationships is imperative to a refugee's mental, emotional, social, and physical health. GMOs like World Relief practice holistic healing, creating programs such as cultural companions to help refugees and asylees navigate everyday life upon their arrival, and community gardens where refugees can congregate with other refugees to grow community and access familiar food to consume.

Durga and Phauda sit beside their garden in the scant shade of a small tree as they tell their story. It has been seven years since their arrival in the US. Though there are hard days, they have found joy where they were planted once again.

Durga murmurs with thankfulness for the health care provided to them. "Two years ago, Phauda [had] open heart surgery." The problem had started 11 years ago, and now he was finally able to get treatment. They spend their days teaching their grandchildren how they used to farm in Bhutan, and about their cultural heritage. "They are light." Durga smiles wistfully. She loves to pick marigolds with them, her favorite flower. She looks forward to teaching her granddaughters to braid their hair—hair they will never have to cut.

"

It was our only option. That time was very hard, because I could
not speak the English and could not understand.

"

"*Durga*"
20"x30" Watercolor

"*Marigold*"
14"x14" Watercolor

"*Durga in the Garden*"
14"x14" Watercolor

"*Durga and Phauda*"
14"x14" Watercolor

VALENTYNA OSTAPETS

UKRAINE

Valentyna's shoes clack quietly up the sidewalk alongside her two coworkers. Stopping before the entryway of the apartment, she shuffles state documents and papers, double-checking the address before rapping on the door. A medium-built woman answers, wiping flour from her hands while children bustle about her skirts. The whole family is new to America.

"Hello!" greets Valentyna, "Are Yulia and Ivan here? I'm their caseworker from World Relief. We are here to help you get settled into your new home." Recognition lights up the woman's face. Warmly, she motions Valentyna into a packed living room. The fragrance wafting from "welcome home bouquets" embraces Valentyna while boisterous Ukrainian conversations tickle her ear. A thrill of nostalgia enveloped her. The scampering little voices followed by chastising parents made Valentyna's heart ache for simpler days, spending mornings with her sisters picking flowers in her families' garden.

Twenty-nine years ago, six-year-old Valentyna awoke to the bellowing voice of her father, "Valentyna, Katya, Ira! Time to wake up, loves!"

Valentyna groaned, futilely rubbing the sleep from her eyes. "Why is it," she sighed, "that normal children get to sleep in their beds, and we have to get up to cut flowers?" She plopped her pillow over her face, blocking the intruding summer light. Her two sisters murmured their solidarity, half-stepping, half-stumbling into their garden clothes. As an adult, Valentyna would look back fondly at their morning ritual. "At five AM, I needed to go with my sister to cut the flowers because my mom and dad would go to the farmer market and sell them."

Rows of glistening gems greeted her as the sun kissed each bead of morning dew. Kneeling, she fell into the familiar "thwack, thwack, thwack" of cutting the gladiolas. Her mind drifted to the mound of dishes she would have to clean later, scheming up ways to get out of it.

"I HATED doing dishes so I hid them. I was kind of lazy girl," chuckled Valentyna. "My dad laughed many years later getting the treasures I hid in the garden."

Valentyna stifled a yawn. She was, and still is, a natural optimist, but early mornings and dishes were not among her passions.

What Valentyna did get excited about were words. "I loved to tell poems in church on Sunday," she smiles, remembering. Her family were members of an Evangelical Christian church. Valentyna grew up during the end of Soviet Union rule, when religion of any kind was prohibited. "Every Sunday we have guest come in and share their stories about jail, how their families were killed. My grandma lost her job because she was believer," remembers Valentyna. Though she never met her grandma, her brave legacy lives on through her family.

Valentyna and her family had to be careful about every word or action they shared so they might avoid persecution. This was hard for Valentyna, as her exuberant and social personality naturally drew her to share with those around her.

She remembers one Sunday when the pastor at her church gave her a beautiful new book about the Biblical story of Jonah. "It was really so beautiful, bright, and SO colorful." She recalled, "I wanted to share with my friends." Books, particularly new books, were a rarity in Ukraine. Eager to share her treasure with her classmates, she excitedly skipped up the school steps cradling the book. Later that day, the teacher sharply instructed Valentyna to hide the book. The principal spoke with Valentyna's mother, forbidding her or her family to talk about God, and that if she continued, they would have to expel her. The experience left Valentyna's gentle heart crushed. How

could something she had done out of such joy, of her own volition, cause such hostility? The gossip from her classmates worsened because of this event. They called her "shtunda," a derogatory name for a Christian. This is only one of many trials Valentyna faced because of her faith.

When Valentyna was 22, she began her master's program working towards a Ph.D. in law. Her warm and high-spirited personality continued to draw people like a magnet. Instantly, she made friends with her classmates and professors, opening her room for social gatherings.

One typical day, chatting with a fellow classmate, Valentyna casually invited a friend to a play at a local church. Her heartfelt invitation was cut short by an abrupt "shht" from her friend, accentuated by a single finger pressed to his lips.

"Don't talk about that. Don't invite anyone to church," he hissed. "People talk. They say you do bad things in church —force conversion on people." He went on to explain that her seemingly amiable professors were secretly investigating Valentyna behind her back to find cause for expulsion so they would not have a "shtunda" among them.

"

Things have changed so much because of the war in the East.

"

Taken aback by her dear friend's sudden transformation, a cold, prickling hurt began to set heavily in her heart. Realization of the continued betrayal crushed Valentyna. "I didn't even have power to cry." She relented, "I don't get it. It's not honest. They know me. Why not talk directly with me, I have nothing to hide. I didn't want to be in the same situation my grandmother was in and lose my job because of my faith. But if it's needed for God's glory, I will – even if it's not fair."

As Valentyna finished up her Ph.D., life became increasingly more difficult. The war in Ukraine and political instability put Valentyna's future at risk, particularly because of her position in law. As the Orthodox Church began gaining influence in eastern Ukraine, persecution of those who were not Orthodox, including Protestants, increased. Valentyna's family urged her to apply for resettlement as a refugee. "Things have changed so much because of the war in the East." Says Valentyna, "My friends have died... pastors, students. You never know what could happen tomorrow. Ukraine is small country so it could come to your work, your house, any day." She applied for refugee status on the grounds of religious persecution. Though she was elated that her request was accepted, matters quickly became more complicated due to unforeseen circumstances.

Valentyna's father had been battling cancer. Upon Valentyna's acceptance as a refuge, her family received news that his health was taking a turn for the worse and he only had a few months to live. She spent every waking moment caring for her father, and was torn between staying with her family and seeking refuge in America.

One morning, she declared to her father that she would stay in Ukraine to take care of him. The shadow of his once-strong hand embraced hers as he looked her in the eye. With a gentle firmness that only a father can muster, he told her that he wanted a better future for her, and that he would be happier if she were safe in America. She looked down at his hand encircling hers. Memories of soccer games, Sunday picnics, and parading the streets hand in hand pushed at the back of her eyes. "Holding your hand," she whispered past the lump in her throat, "and being your daughter is much more important than all the treasures in the world."

"

It's not like you can say, 'oh don't worry we will see each other'.
Because we understand we will not.

"

That night the house was silent as she packed her few belongings for America. "We didn't know what to say." She remembers. "It's not like you can say, 'Oh don't worry we will see each other.' Because we understand we will not. You just hug, and hold each other."

With 50 dollars in her pocket and little else, Valentyna boarded a plane to America.

Going from a bright career in Law after earning her Ph.D. to a sales clerk at David's Bridal was difficult. But Valentyna was determined to make her way. Navigating a new culture, language, currency, climate and life was dizzying. "I think it's especially hard for independent people who had career and good education back in their countries. It's hard to depend on somebody. You literally can't do anything without somebody's navigation. You feel disabled, stupid, frustrated and paralyzed." For the first few weeks, Valentyna felt so discouraged and cumbersome, that all she wanted to do was pack her bags and go home, but she couldn't. Slowly but surely, with the help of World Relief and many others, she began to make her way in this new life. After going through World Relief herself, they asked her to join their team as a caseworker, helping other refugees and asylees. It was the perfect opportunity for Valentyna to unabashedly and freely help others with a team of support behind her.

Current day, in the living room of Yulia and Ivan, through paperwork, a drive to the DSHS, and countless grandchildren that wriggle in Yulia and Ivan's arms, Valentyna bonds with the sweet elderly couple. Excitedly, she speaks of yearning for her own big Ukrainian family one day.

As they finish up for the day, Ivan leans forward with quiet confidence, looking Valentyna in the eye, he took her hand, "You are angel of our family. Thank you." Valentyna reciprocates the action. Difficult days are ahead of this family, but they will not be alone.

"Valentyna"
16"x20" Watercolor

"Valentyna at Work"
16"x20" Watercolor

AHMAD ZUBAIR

AFGHANISTAN

"

They looked at the metals, the jewelry and the American flags. He was not given a chance, there was no judge...My brother was killed.

"

Ahmad ducked behind the dashboard just as the second bullet sliced through the window. His ears rang with the impact and his heart slammed against his chest. Fear trickled in rivulets down his back. The Taliban had come to make good on their threats. Another shot came. This time he heard his cousin cry out in pain as he held his shoulder where the bullet hit. They sped away, barely escaping with their lives.

The two cousins were on their way to their boutique in Afghanistan when they were ambushed. The Taliban had found out that they, as well as Ahmad's brother, sold their handmade products to American soldiers—a connection that was forbidden under the Taliban.

The Taliban is a fundamentalist Islamic military group whose aim is to enforce their extreme interpretation of Sharia law. Under the Taliban, any foreign influence or beliefs that do not align with their own radical ones are eliminated by violence and terrorist acts. This was the third of three attacks on their family. The first happened to Ahmad's brother while he was delivering inventory to one of the nearby jewelry shops.

"They stopped him and checked his car," Ahmad would say later, his characteristic smile melting to a somber air as he recalled the memory. "They looked at the metals, the jewelry and [American] flags. He was not given a chance, there was no judge... My brother was killed...after, they throw him in the street." Ahmad was forced to close down their family's boutique, in hopes that they would be left alone.

Ahmad stood in his empty shop, packing up the last of his belongings. He could not take everything with him. He looked forlornly at the heirloom tools that would now collect dust in his absence. Memories of life in the shop danced before his eyes. He saw his grandfather's weathered hands encircling his inexperienced ones as he taught seven-year-old Ahmad how to run the shop. He remembered the hum of customers, deliberating over which necklace to buy for their sweetheart back home.

The only remaining evidence of the last few years would be his memories and the squares of clean pressed carpet where tables and cabinets once stood. For Ahmad, it had never been about the money: he lived for the relationships. His dimply smile put everyone at ease as they

laughed, reminisced, and imagined the future over a warm dish of homemade Palau. Ahmad's warm Muslim family opened their home and table to all their customers, no matter their nationality or religion. They were like family.

With a final clank, Ahmad locked the door behind him.

His whole family scattered, fleeing for their lives as they found refuge in various countries. Ahmad was able to get a tourist visa to America. With a heavy heart, he bid his home farewell and boarded a plane.

As time passed, Ahmad realized it was still unsafe for him to return to Afghanistan. The reality that he might never be able to return home, began to sink in. Soon Ahmad was arrested for overstaying his visa. Tears washed over him as he was transported to the car in leg, arm, and neck shackles. "I wasn't trying to be problem. I was just thinking, I want to go somewhere safe." Unable to speak or understand English, it was hours of interrogation before they passed him off to ICE (Department of Homeland Security Immigration and Customs Enforcement). He was less worried after an interpreter explained to him what had taken place

and what would happen next. In order to stay long term, he would have to prove his need for asylum, and until then, he would stay in a detention center.

In the detention center, Ahmad had a hard time adjusting to the sheer mass of people around him and the size of the building. He felt like he was in prison, similar to the movies he saw when he was younger, complete with itchy uniforms and tasteless food.

"Every day was beans," exclaims Ahmad, his expressive eyes growing large. "Lunch was beans and night was beans. Every day is beans!" He laughs, slapping his knee. "I was thinking, people ask 'What's your name?' I say, MY NAME IS BEANS." After nine months in these conditions, Ahmad was finally able to obtain asylum status in the United States.

"I felt like a small baby," recalls Ahmad, when asked about his first few days free, but alone in the United States. He was soon referred to World Relief, where they helped him get a job and an apartment. He quickly knit together a community of friends and family. As they helped him get on his feet, he wanted to do the same for others. He began teaching craft design

"

I wasn't trying to be problem... I was thinking I want to go somewhere safe.

"

to refugee women so that they too could make a living.

Two years later, Ahmad sits on his couch after a long day of work. He waits for his sister to call him. It is Ramadan and its nights like this that he misses his family most. As dusk fell, his family would open their homes as they ended their fast together. He remembers the intoxicating scent of his mother's cooking, the jests of his siblings, and the satisfaction of working beside his cousin. Though his heart aches, he knows he is safe. He breathes a sigh of thankfulness, dreaming of a day when he will get to be with his family again.

"Ahmad"
16"x20" Watercolor

"Ahmad's Jewlery"
16"x20" Watercolor

These paintings have been cropped to protect the subjects identity.

JEANNE D'ARC MUSABYIMANA

RWANDA

"

I wished to stay in village, I wished to finish my school... and have good family... And I got it, but with the war, everything changed.

"

"I remember when I was young," says Jeanne with a bittersweet smile.

The sunlight streaks through the blinds of her home, highlighting the gold flecks in her dark eyes. She fidgets with the hem of her wax fabric, as she recalls a distant memory. "Every day I told my mom that I have to be big person."

Jeanne wanted to be just like her mother, a Rwandan marriarch with a warm, bustling home, where no company went home hungry or lonely. A new mother herself, Jeanne was eager to follow in her mother's footsteps. "I wished to stay in village, I wished to finish my school... and have good family... And I got it. But with the war, everything changed."

Rumors of political discontentment between the Hutu and Tutsi tribes began to spread. The whispers cast a foreboding shadow on her new role as a wife and a mother.

"Before the war... Tutsi and Hutus lived in peace together," she explains. While her husband was away for work, Jeanne stayed home, huddled close to her one-year-old son, rubbing her growing belly. As the due date for her second child drew near, she prayed for the tension to dissipate.

Little did she know that their country was on the precipice of the fastest widespread slaughter in history that would soon force her away from her mother and family. When the president's plane was hit by a missile, all hell broke loose.

"That is where it all started," whispers Jeanne, "the long journey of the darkest days of my life."

On the morning of April 7, 1994, civil war broke out between the Hutu and Tutsi tribes. Blood ran through the streets as people were slaughtered in their homes.

"Anyone who appeared to be Tutsi was killed without hesitation." Determined to save her family, she tied her son securely around her back. She could feel his body trembling against her back as his sobs mingled with the curdling cries of neighbors. On swollen feet, she ran with hundreds of other civilians towards the shelter of the trees in the Congo rainforest, hoping to find refuge in the Congo. When the soles of her feet began to bleed, still she pressed on. "I was in so much pain...I fought my limits because I found a reason to persevere and that was my babies... the little boy I was carrying on my back and the one in my womb... my entire existence had lost the taste of

hope for myself." As they trekked on, hunger, thirst, and infection caused by the wounds from the massacre began to claim its victims one by one. Cries from men, women, and children were soon replaced by the deafening silence of death.

"Many people lost sisters and brothers, I also lost family members." Night and day, people were killed, violence coming from every corner. "Each day felt like a year... I was so young, and the world took so much away from me. But God never stopped watching over me." During those dark days, her faith in God brought her hope.

Over the span of 100 days, over 70% of the Tutsi population in Rwanda was massacred in addition to many Hutu civilians. Like thousands of other Rwandans, Jeanne sought asylum in a refugee camp on the borders of the Congo, but it came with a cost.

"All around there was complete destruction...we were living like animals in the forest. Cholera and diarrhea killed many refugees in the camp." Amidst the smells of sewage ripe in the air and contaminated water, Jeanne brought her second son into the world. She prayed that God would save them. Jeanne's prayers were answered when she and her children were reunited with her husband.

Jeanne and her husband found a place to live in the Congo, where they ran a boutique to support their growing family. Jeanne gave birth to three more children, a girl named Aimée, and twins named Boris and Ghislain. As her babies took their first steps, Jeanne felt like a newborn herself, shakily learning to navigate everyday life after trauma.

"I felt the urge to quickly heal, because I didn't want my kids to be associated with the horrific war. I didn't want to take the innocence from them like the world had done to me." Though she kept her grief quiet, some images are engraved in her mind. Jeanne confesses, "I still live some of those days every night when I go to bed. They haunt me." Amidst the pain, Jeanne's resolution to fight for a better life for her children only grew stronger. "It was these little humans' smiles that warmed my heart and gave it a new reason to keep beating." Soon, she would need that resolution to overcome a second hardship.

In 2006, Jeanne and her husband divorced, as the stress of survival took a toll on their marriage. From then on, Jeanne alone cared for her five children. Without child support or help from the government, Jeanne worked tirelessly putting her children through school and providing for their everyday needs.

"It was very difficult being a single woman with five kids," Jeanne admits. Overcome with love, she added, "Living for them is an honor for me. I have chosen to raise them with love, and fear nothing." Aimée, her daughter, recalls memories of her mother denying food so that she and her brothers could eat. "Because my mom was positive, she didn't want you to see that she wasn't eating, but I saw it... It was hard watching my mom work so hard." Even as children, Aimée and her siblings followed in their mom's selfless footsteps, working hard to please her and take care of their family. Though they had little, Aimée remembers saving up the meager pennies she earned to buy food for her neighbors in need. Aimée promised her mom and herself one day, "I will never give up on my dreams and to make you happy."

Though the conditions in the Congo were safer than Rwanda, survival was a daily struggle. Refugees were treated differently, and often derogatorily. "It wasn't our country," says Aimée, "We were called outsiders even though we were born there." Though Jeanne and her children struggled with their identity, Aimée and her siblings grew up embracing Congolese culture as their own. Barely scraping by, Jeanne knew that the Congo was only a temporary solution if her children were to have a future.

In 2003, Jeanne had applied for refugee status through the UNHCR. For 10 years, Jeanne faithfully attended tedious health screenings, interviews, and applications, her five children in tow. Every year they waited to no avail. Finally, in 2013, she was informed that the UNHCR was placing her family in a foreign land she had yet to hear of—Seattle, Washington.

Though Jeanne was apprehensive and fearful of starting over for the third time, she could feel the hum of opportunity for her children as she landed in the United States. Her children, too, felt the relief.

"After years of fear and instability, we were excited to come to this land of opportunity that we can now call home," Aimée says, brimming with gratitude. "Here we have started a new life—though it has not been easy."

Simple things like going to school, grocery shopping, answering the door or eating American foods came at Jeanne's family, a tidal wave of change. Aimée remembers feeling overwhelmed at first. "I was having to navigate a new culture, language and even the food at lunchtime was terrifying. I would practice English words at home so I could speak clearly and began to join extracurricular clubs." World Relief helped Jeanne and her children navigate these

"

It was these little human's smiles that warmed my heart and gave it
a new reason to keep beating.

"

changes and are a continued support in their lives.

Currently, three of Jeanne's children attend university and two have graduated with degrees in civil engineering and environmental science – something they had only dreamt about before, now, a reality. The tables have turned. Today, Jeanne's children work tirelessly to make their mother proud, and it is her smile that gives them reason to keep going.

Ghislain wrote in an essay, "Seeing my mom and her motivation...that will always be with me wherever I go. I may not always have the skills...but with drive and motivation, nothing is gonna stop me...I want to give back to kids like me, because God has given us so much." Jeanne has raised her children with the same principles of love and hospitality that her mom taught her. Aimée speaks with a fiery determination, "I carry on with a warrior spirit that was instilled in me...Changing legacies and affecting the future take a special kind of courage, I know because I have my mother's example to follow."

Jeanne is often tired from working nights, but she is content. "Although my journey has not been what I expected as a child, today I can say that my heart is at peace.

God never ceased to be there by my side." Jeanne works with World Relief, helping refugees like herself, and opening her home to anyone in need. She is, "... a matriarch with a warm, bustling home, where no company went home hungry or lonely," just like her mother. Devastatingly, Jeanne's mother passed away before she was able to return to Rwanda to see her again. Finding solace in carrying on her legacy through herself and her children, she continues to love and care for those around her.

"Jeanne"
16"x20" Watercolor

"Aimée"
16"x20" Watercolor

"Ghislain and Boris"
20"x30" Watercolor

ABDULLAH BIN YAKOOB

MYANMAR

Abdullah grins, watching his nine-month-old son Umair as he claps his chubby hands over his mother's cheeks, mimicking the "kissy-face" she is making at him. Khadijah, Abdullah's wife, holds her wriggly son as he grasps his father's finger and offers up a small smile.

Back in Myanmar, there are people who wish that Umair didn't exist. People who would make it their main mission to extinguish the light in Umair's eyes forever.

Abdullah grew up in Yangon, Myanmar. At five years old, a boy like him might have painstakingly scrawled out the first few letters of his name, then frozen, as the realization of his mistake washed over him. It wasn't safe to write his real name at school.

As he frantically erased, the boy would look over his shoulder to make sure his classmates didn't notice his blunder. Walking home, he would hardly notice the vendors, busses, and cattle shoving past him, replaying his slip-up over and over to the pounding of his feet, hoping there was not punishment at school waiting for him tomorrow.

"In my school I could not use my name," Abdullah explains. "They said, 'You must use a Buddhist name.'" Abdullah was forbidden to talk about or show any part of his Rohingyan Muslim heritage, including his birth name. "In Myanmar they don't accept Rohingya... Buddhist are a majority. They hold the power and discriminate against other religions. Buddhists got all the higher level jobs. They keep citizenship from Rohingya." Extremist Buddhist terrorist groups have burned out Rohingya villages, massacred people and blocked roads so they couldn't escape.

Solemnly, Abdullah recalled the bitter taste of living in perpetual fear in his village. "I have family and friends that go outside and have fear... At night time, they (Buddhist terrorist groups) come and throw the stone and make the noise. They want to make violence. They call us Kala [a derogatory racial slur for Muslims]." Years of tension and conflict between Myanmar Buddhists and Rohingya has led to one of the most globally overlooked genocides and ethnic cleansing today.

Rohingya Muslims are an ethnoreligious group whose settlement in the North Rakhine State of Myanmar (formerly

Burma) dates as far back as the 1400s. Though many of the Rohingya's roots go back longer than some of their Buddhist neighbors, Rohingyas are labeled "illegals" and "criminals" in their own home and country. A lasting, violent tension wrought from nationalism and Islamophobia has now led to extreme systematic discrimination and full on genocide in recent years. Rohingya Muslims are sent to forced labor camps and suffer rape, torture, and summary executions. There has been a mass exodus of nearly 700,000 Rohingya Muslims in the last decade, fleeing to Bangladesh, South East Asia, and parts of the Middle East, desperate for survival. While some are able to find other opportunities like Abdullah, most are stuck in another kind of death sentence. With nowhere to go, generations of displaced Rohingyas are now being born into disease, extreme poverty, and addiction as a result of overflowing refugee camps with no medical aid, running water, or electricity.

Abdullah was one of the few who was able to pursue schooling and work as a technician in Malaysia. Still, he was limited since he could not become a legal citizen. It was there he met and eventually married Khadijah, his hardworking and detail-oriented wife, who gave birth to their first two children Syihaabeddiin and Azizah. At that time, though conditions were quickly worsening, the extremity of ethnic cleansing had not yet reached their home country of Myanmar. Rapidly decreasing civil rights in Malaysia, however, foreshadowed the impending massacre. The daily fear of being sent back to Myanmar was very real for their family, especially since they desired to grow their family once again. The Myanmar government had restricted Rohingya families to no more than two children. Violation of this law would invite severe punishment on the child and his family. If they were to have a third child, they would need to reach a place of permanence and safety.

In 2013, Abdullah applied for refugee status through the UNHCR (The United Nations High Commissioner for Refugees). He knew it was a long shot as that out of over 25 million refugees, less than one percent are resettled.

Shock and relief swept over him when he received the news telling him that he and his family were to be relocated to a town called Kent, Washington in the United States of America.

"

I have family and friends that go outside and have fear... At night time, they come and throw the stone and make the noise. They want to make violence.

"

World Relief aided the Abdullah family through the trauma of acclimating to a new culture and healing from a life of uncertainty and oppression. "My family is very thank you for the World Relief. When I come here I don't know nothing," expressed Abdullah fervently. "We got letters and not know what they were. We went to World Relief and they help understand how to pay bill and paperwork in America." Abdullah secured a job working for maintenance at the Hilton Hotel while his wife worked at Costco. Soon, Khadijah took maternity leave for the arrival of their third child, Umair, a testament of the newly found freedom and refuge they had at last found for their family.

Present day, in the living room of Abdullah's apartment in Kent, Umair clasps his father's finger tightly, feeling emboldened in the safe embrace of his parents' arms. Abdullah gazes warmly at his wife and third child—a reality he still finds hard to believe. Umair, and children like him, are the reason parents and countless other refugees risk death at sea or foot, so that they can write their birth name at school, and go home with no fear.

"Abdullah"
16"x20" Watercolor

"Khadijah and Azizah"
16"x20" Watercolor

"Bedroom"
14"x14" Watercolor

"Khadijah and Umair"
20"x30" Watercolor

HELEN MEHARI

ERITREA

"

I heard about America.... That they help people that are immigrants.

"

Helen burst into her family's shop, letting the weight of a full day of lectures roll off her shoulders and onto the counter with her school books. The aroma of fresh baked bread enveloped her in a cocoon, mingling with the crisp scent of holiday grasses decorating the shop.

"Smells like harmony," she thought, breathing deeply.

Easter was fast approaching, and her mother was in a frenzy preparing their grocery store for their eager customers. Her mother shouted from the kitchen in the back, "Helen, is that you?"

Helen found her mom wrestling over a fresh cut of veal. After leaning in for a quick kiss, Helen popped into the room she shared with her three brothers and changed out of her school uniform. This had become routine since her father passed away a few years ago, when her mother bought the shop as a means of supporting their family.

There is not a day that goes by when Helen doesn't miss her father.

"He made my mother laugh, all of us laugh. He was close to family, always having people over. He was hard worker, people always say he was brilliant," Helen would later say.

Like all Eritrean citizens, her father was forced to conscribe to the Eritrean military service as a soldier. Conscription to the military in Eritrea leaves the term "soldier" wanting, as harsh conditions render the position more accurately described as a slave.

At sixteen years old, Eritrean citizens are registered for mandatory military school followed by at least one year of service, or, as in the case of Helen's father, indefinitely. Consequences for not complying with these laws are often punishable by imprisonment and torture, both to the offender and the offender's family.

Helen was nine years old when her family received the news that her father wouldn't be coming home. He had died in combat. Helen and her family were left to fend for themselves in a country with an economy and environment that was increasingly hostile.

Since Eritrea's independence from Ethiopia in 1991, its citizens continue to be shaken by continuous bouts of war and conflict. The country's borders and media became increasingly restricted. Along with North Korea, Eritrea is rated lowest in freedom rankings for global media. Not only does the government control almost every aspect of adult citizens' lives, it is also involved in some of the worst forms of child labor. Stunted advancement in education, economy, and agriculture has led Eritrea to be one of the poorest countries in Africa.

At age 24, it became clear to Helen that she needed to earn more than the meager wages she earned from her government-sanctioned job to help support her family.

"The government makes people struggle. With military, there's no freedom in Eritrea. Once you graduate you can't work wherever you want, you can't choose where you go. They choose where you go," explains Helen. With a showering of kisses and tearful goodbyes, Helen left Eritrea for Sudan. It was hard leaving her family. She spoke of her mother particularly, "She always motivating to be strong and be good person. To pursue my passions.... Without family I was scared what's next. I realize God protect me wherever I go."

In Sudan, Helen was welcomed into an artist community where she was offered a job teaching art to other immigrants. It was there she nurtured a love for art, and discovered her passion for helping others. While she loved her job, living in Sudan became increasingly complicated and brought its own set of risks.

Not being a Sudanese citizen and practicing her Christian faith in a Muslim country put a target on Helen's back. Rogue troops, operating under the guise of Sudan police, took advantage of immigrants and their families. They detained migrants under the pretense that they did not have proper paperwork.

"They ask for a lot of money, we pay for the paper, they never give us the paper." Helen recalled, "I just wanted to be somewhere safe..." she whispered. "I heard about America.... That they help people that are immigrants." Worsening conditions in Sudan forced Helen to make the abrupt decision to embark on a journey crossing 11 countries and an ocean in hopes of seeking asylum in America.

Harrowing obstacles and victories in her six month journey across the Atlantic Ocean and up through South America left an imprint on Helen's heart. There were times where she and other immigrants spent nights without food or water in the Amazon jungle, or crossed countries where people met their plea with hostility and aggression. But there were also times when people countered Helen's loneliness with open arms and understanding, giving her food, water, and companionship. Forever the brave optimist, Helen smiled ruefully saying, "It was like a risky vacation."

Approaching the border from Mexico to the United States, Helen was surprised at the size and amount of security, "There were a lot of American soldiers. We give them our immigration papers. People came to meet us and took us in and asked a lot of questions to verify who we are and where we are from … searched our hair, our shoes, and our clothes… to verify who we are and where we are from." After determining that Helen was not a threat, the US military sent her to a detention center in Bakersfield, California.

Five months later, Helen sat in a small fluorescent-lit room awaiting the judge's verdict at the detention center. She was grateful that the trial was over video so that she could conceal her trembling hands under the table. Though she was well cared for in the detention center, the five months of mental and emotional stress in purgatory felt like eternity. As with most migrants, Helen had no funds or means to hire an attorney and was at the mercy of pro bono volunteers to take up her case. People often had to wait years for the opportunity. "Nobody can pay for me. I was praying someone would help me," said Helen.

She was stunned when she got a call from Julia, an attorney who, inspired by her story, offered to represent Helen's case pro bono. As Helen unfolded her story, Julia and Helen wept together bonding over Helen's harrowing obstacles and hard-earned victories. Julia sat beside her, now with a translator and another immigration officer in the small room. Dwarfed by the large screen in front of them, they sat waiting for the judge to grant or deny Helen's plea for asylum.

Questions and doubts thrummed through Helen's ears. "Did I answer the questions correctly? Will they believe me? "Oh God," she prayed, "I crossed 11 countries and an ocean, is this my end?" Helen snapped back realizing the judge was looking at her expectantly "—can—can you please repeat, your honor?" she stammered. Had she addressed him correctly?

"Yesterday was your birthday?" repeated the judge.

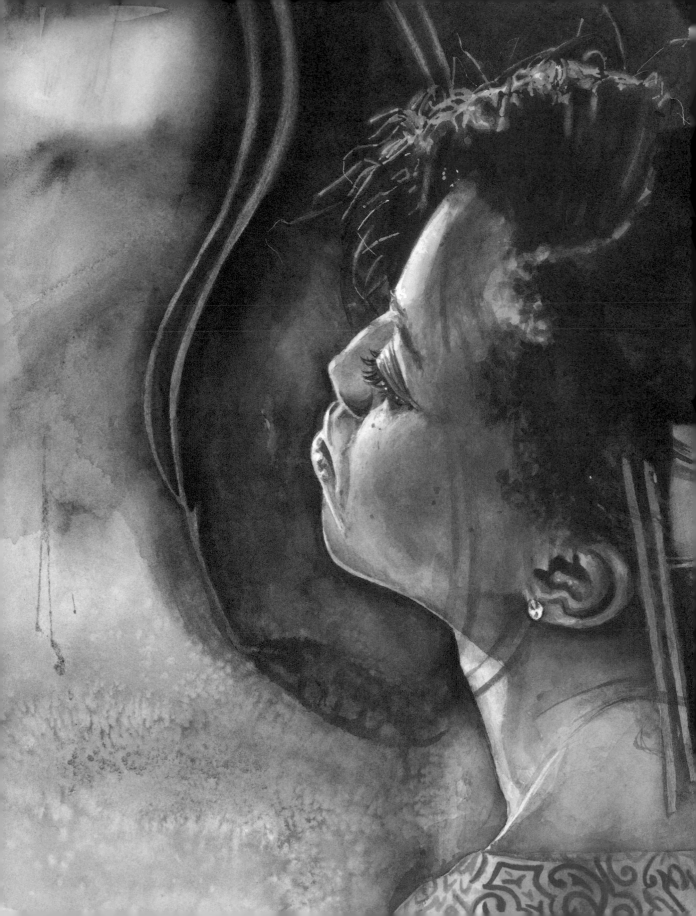

"

It was like I was born again. I feel freedom.

"

"Yes. I turn 26, your honor," responded Helen.

"Well, Happy Birthday, Helen...I grant you asylum in the United States of America."

Waves of relief spilled over her, dousing the flames of doubts, fears, and anxieties she had stoked over the years. Had she heard him correctly? Was she really safe? The immigration officer passed her a tissue to dab at the relief spilling down her cheeks. For the first time in her life she was free. She no longer was an oppressed citizen, on the run, or a detainee. She was an asylee in the United States of America.

Helen stepped out of the detention center buzzing with anticipation. Feeling the familiar bend of her jeans instead of the government issued uniforms, she heard the final clank of the barbed wire cyclone fence shutting behind her. The air was charged with sunlight, splashing warmth on her face and arms. Closing her eyes, she took her first breath of fresh air as a free person.

"It was like I was born again. I feel freedom," remembered Helen. "I had bright eyes, darting everywhere. I didn't even ride a car, touch a phone for five months." Ahead of her, she saw someone waving her down from a white vehicle. Helen rushed towards Julia in an embrace. They had done it. Helen had told her story and she was safe. "God is still with me. He is working on me. Wherever I go, He is protecting me." One last time she looked back at the cyclone barbed wire fence saying a prayer for the sisterhood of migrants and asylum seekers that had become her family. While she was at the tail end of her journey through hell, many of the others had just begun. She prayed for kind and understanding hearts to intervene in their lives as Julia had hers.

It was a long road ahead of her, but for the first time her future was a blank canvas where she could decide the strokes. Prospects of nursing school, attending church free of persecution, and most of all, her biggest dream of having her family safe beside her, peeked over the horizon.

"Helen Drawing"
16"x20" Watercolor

"Helen"
16"x20" Watercolor

ALAN ABDULLAH

IRAQ

"

Our city was safe... until ISIS showed up.

"

Alan placed his hand on two-month-old Aleen's back as she drifted in and out of sleep. His other hand held up his head as he slumped in a chair beside her crib. Tonight had been a particularly bad bout of labored breathing for her. Aleen's body shook with rasping breaths. Alan lit up the screen of his phone, checking the time. In a couple of hours, he would go to the American military base, where he worked as a translator in Kirkuk, Iraq. This was one of three jobs, barely keeping his family afloat amidst the medical bills and living expenses. He stood and leaned his head towards his little girl, kissing the curls on the back of her head, sweaty from a fitful sleep. He prayed once again that God would spare her life, and that they would find answers.

Alan and his wife Nasha took Aleen to countless doctors, their two-year-old son Aland in tow. From Iraq to India, to Turkey, doctors uttered the same prognoses: "borrowed time," "will not live," "no cure." The doctor would pass along yet another pill that might extend their daughter's life, or more likely, be a scam with a fancy price tag. Soon, Aleen's mother, Nasha, was diagnosed with the same rare heart condition as her daughter.

"That's when everyone broke in my family," says Alan years later. "Especially my wife. She started losing her faith. That's when I really thought I have to leave this country.... The healthcare was really bad."

Little did they know that an extremist militant group called ISIS would soon add another threat to their family.

"Our city was safe... until ISIS showed up," explains Alan. "It was a surprise to us... we didn't have an idea what ISIS was or where they came from." ISIS had set up camp just an hour from their home. Most of the time ISIS was kept out, but the times they got through, the group left a trail of slaughter, taking hostage the few that were spared. Alan recalls keeping bags packed at all times in case they had to flee at a moment's notice.

Alan's position as a Muslim civilian working for the American Army made him a primary target for ISIS. Alan was born to a Sunni Muslim home, living peacefully amongst friends of various faiths. With a crease in his brow, he sternly spoke of ISIS, frustration and hurt clearly stirring him. "ISIS pretends to be Muslim. They play the Muslim card as entry into uneducated areas to fulfill their agenda and make their own rules, and make money... People say they are Muslim. They are not Muslim.

We are Muslim. Go behind the picture. It [ISIS' agenda] is business... I pray to God ISIS lose...because if they won't, they will just keep going."

Alan and Nasha are passionate about teaching their children the Quran so that they can discern who is using their religion for nefarious purposes and will not be caught unawares. Living by example, Alan and Nasha teach their little ones that, "It doesn't matter what color you are, doesn't matter what religion, you must treat people with respect and welcome them." Alan adds, "That is how humanity will continue."

Alan began the process of acquiring a visa to America at the American Embassy in Bagdad. Though Alan would normally have driven to Bagdad, he was forced to fly, because ISIS had taken control of the roads. Only because of his position in the military did the process to obtain a visa take one year instead of multiple. He was lucky. The health of his wife and daughter could not have waited longer.

Alan and his family arrived in America in 2016. They were immediately sent to the Seattle Children's Hospital, where they began testing Nasha and Aleen, treating their symptoms. It was soon found out that Aland, their oldest son, also had a mild version of the genetic disease.

"I really appreciate living in the US, especially Washington State," Alan says emphatically, "because of healthcare providing for my kids and wife. When I was back home I could not afford it. I was working three jobs... at home, I wasn't getting even one one-thousandth of the care we are getting here."

Though his family's health was still at high risk and could turn at any second, treatments and medications stabilized the disease so it would not worsen. "They are alive. They are safe. They will grow up with a healthy environment, and [have] a good quality of life as much as possible."

It seemed their life would finally settle down when Alan got a call from home. His mother in Iraq was suffering medically. He was torn. "I have these three people of my blood and also my mom, I didn't know what to do." Reluctant to leave his family, he made plans to visit Iraq for two weeks to care for his mother and come right back in the arms of his wife and children.

Though he was apprehensive about leaving his family in the condition they were in, it was also good to be in his childhood home again. He walked the streets with the familiar smells and chatter, sleeping on the same mat and spot on the floor he grew up with. A few days into his visit, he was abruptly woken by a phone call.

Groggily, he answered, hearing his wife's panicked voice on the other end telling him to check the news.

The newly elected president of the United States had enforced a travel ban restricting entry from multiple countries, including Iraq where Alan was staying, for at least 90 days.

"At first, I just laughed. I said 'That's impossible'," Alan remembered. "About six hours later, they started stopping people at the airport and that's when I realized it was real."

His heart hammered inside his chest as he swallowed the truth; he would be away from his family indefinitely. A few friends from World Relief contacted him about the situation as well, doing everything on their end, including visiting his wife and children in the states and making calls to Congress.

Alan shakes his head and recalls, "It was scary; I had never been so scared in my life...I got shot twice in the army. That was nothing for me. But if you are a dad, and they keep you away from your family for no reason, that was hard."

'What if?' thoughts began feasting on Alan's mind. What if the medical treatments don't work and my family takes a turn for the worse? What if ISIS finds his children are left vulnerable without a father? In danger where he was, and prohibited from going home, he got to work exhausting every avenue to get to his family.

Hoping that his refugee status, visa, and standing in the American military would push him through, he flew to the American Embassy in Bagdad. He was met with a resounding, "No," though sympathy shown in their eyes. The very country he had taken two bullets for would not let him come home.

Waving his hands, he recalls, "No one knew what was going on. No one knew what was going to happen. And no one knew for how long." Throwing the dice, Alan posted his story on Facebook. Not expecting a response, he heard dings resounding from his phone of shares, likes, and comments as people heard his story. World Relief and others had begun making calls to Congress pleading on his behalf. A Canadian journalist who heard about his plight wrote an article about him, spreading his story. Within two days, an American lawyer who had heard of his case volunteered to represent him pro bono.

Alan was moved deeply by the mass of people that rallied together to get him home. Even if the plan didn't work, he would forever be changed by the people advocating for him and his family. He was moved by the freedom of speech in America. "In America, nothing is impossible...It's not about who's in power. It's about the people. People make the changes. I saw it. We didn't have those rights [in Iraq]... We didn't have freedom of speech... you would lose your life."

Tentative but full of hope, Alan boarded the plane that would begin his journey home.

At every checkpoint, he trembled as he held out his papers. He was afraid of detainment and another rejection, hoping the paperwork, legal advice, and network of people supporting him in America would be enough to keep him safe. His racing mind forbid him from

sleep during the 14-hour flight to Los Angeles, California, sharing nervous glances with two other families on the plane in a similar predicament.

As the plane jostled and landed, he prepared himself for the inevitable detainment. How long would the interrogations last? What if he can't go home? Where would he end up? The questions played at the back of his mind. As he headed to the holding room, his eyes

fell on the lawyer who had met him at the airport, ready if need be. The door latched behind them.

Without his phone, he had no way to let his family in Iraq or America know what was going on, or if he was safe. Three hours inched by. Four. Alan waited as the officers met with each individual one by one. At last, after five hours, his name was called. He fidgeted in his chair, answering the questions as honestly as possible, and praying that it would be enough. Finally, the words reached his ears, words that he would never forget.

"Welcome home," said the officer as he handed Alan his phone and his passport.

He immediately called his family and lawyer to tell them the good news. Later he would describe the whole experience, shaking his head, "I do not wish for anyone to live that nightmare."

He slipped into the house, closing the door slowly, as to not wake his family. He breathed the familiar smell of dinner lingering into the night, and freshly cleaned laundry. Avoiding creaks in the floor, he crept to his children's bedroom.

"

It doesn't matter what color you are, doesn't matter what religion,
you must treat people with respect and welcome them...That is
how humanity will continue.

"

Tears of thankfulness pricked his eyes as he peered down at their fragile frames beneath the comforter. Aland's face peeked out, and Aleen's curls splashed around her. Out of habit, he reached out and placed his hand on Aleen, listening to her breathe as her back rose and fell under his fingertips.

He slipped into bed beside his sleeping wife. Drifting to sleep, he imagined the small arms of his children that would wrap around him in the morning. They were home, and they were safe—at long last.

"Alan and Aleen"
16"x20" Watercolor

"Nasha and Aleen"
16"x20" Watercolor

"Aland"
16"x20" Watercolor

REFUGEES & ASYLEES

WHO ARE REFUGEES?

According to the US Department of Homeland Security, a refugee is a person outside his or her country of nationality who is unable or unwilling to return to his or her country of nationality because of persecution or a well-founded fear of persecution on account of race, religion, nationality, membership in a particular social group, or political opinion. "Refugee" is a legal status granted by the United Nations High Commissioner for Refugees (UNHCR). Unlike migrants, refugees do not make conscious choices to leave their countries to seek a more prosperous life. Often, they are forced to leave without warning. They must leave behind their homes, most of their belongings, family and friends. They do not have time to plan their travel, say goodbye to loved ones or learn about their new location. The journey to safety for a refugee is full of risks and leaves them vulnerable to disease and abuse. They are not be able to return home unless the situation in their country changes.

WHO ARE ASYLEES?

Asylees are people who meet the definition of refugee, but are already present in the United States or seeking admission at a port of entry. The process for becoming an asylee is complex. Many people apply for asylum in the US either affirmatively or defensively. Affirmative applicants are commonly those who ask for asylum voluntarily or preemptively within the first year of coming to the US. Defensive applicants are commonly those who ask for asylum in response to being apprehended by immigration enforcement.

WHAT ARE REFUGEE CAMPS?

Refugee camps are intended as temporary accommodation for people who have been forced from their homes. They are usually built and run by a government, the United Nations, or non-governmental organizations. When refugees have nowhere else to go, their only chance at survival is coming to a refugee camp in hopes of eventually acquiring resettlement in another country. It can take anywhere from a few years to a lifetime for refugees to finish the resettlement process. While refugee camps are less dangerous than refugees' native homes, they often offer terrible living conditions. They often lack enough water, electricity and food to care for all the people in the overpopulated camps. Disease, rat infestations and contamination often run rampant in the camps and there is little access to healthcare. These refugees are not given the rights of citizenship in the camp host country. There are currently more than 2.6 million people living in refugee camps and many more living in other urban areas throughout the world.

WHAT IS THE RESETTLEMENT PROCESS LIKE?

The goal of the UNHCR is to find solutions to help refugees and asylees rebuild their homes. The first solution is to work towards voluntary repatriation. The second solution is help them integrate into their host community. When the first two solutions are not possible, the final option is to help refugees resettle in another country. Resettlement can be life-saving for refugees all over the world. However, less than 1% of refugees ever obtain resettlement. The United States has one of the largest resettlement programs in the world. The US government has welcomed over 3 million refugees from all over the world for resettlement since the 1970s.

The process for resettlement is long and thorough to help ensure safety. This is the process of resettlement according to the UNHCR:

"In order for a refugee to be resettled, they must first be identified by the UNHCR as a vulnerable case to be referred to resettlement countries. UNHCR collects detailed biographical and biometric data – which may include iris scans, fingerprints and facial scans – for each refugee referred for resettlement. Refugees do not choose their country of resettlement. Persons found to have committed serious crimes or who might pose a threat to others would not be referred for resettlement to another country.

When UNHCR refers a refugee to the US for resettlement, the US government screens the refugee and solely decides whether to admit them to the US for resettlement. This process includes eight government agencies conducting five background checks, six separate security databases and three in-person interviews. This whole process is done abroad and can take more than two years to finish. Once a refugee has been accepted for resettlement, the State Department assigns their case to one of nine US non-governmental organizations (NGO). The selected NGO works closely with partners in the local community to help the refugee find work, integrate and adjust to their new life in the United States."

WORLD RELIEF

More than ever before, vulnerable people around the world are suffering as a result of violence, poverty and injustice. In 2018, there were an unprecedented 68.5 million people around the world who had been forced from their homes. These brave people leave behind everything familiar to seek safety, a life free from fear, and the chance for a new start. Finding themselves in an awful situation, refugees need support.

World Relief is a global Christian humanitarian organization that seeks to provide relief from suffering to refugees and asylees. Through love in action, they bring hope, healing and restoration to the world's most vulnerable people. World Relief serves over 7 million people every year. Each of the refugees interviewed for this book has been a client of World Relief and has greatly benefited from their work.

World Relief offers a number of important services to support refugees and asylees:

- Refugee Resettlement Services support the basic needs of families as they begin a new life in Western Washington.
- Employment Services prepare refugee job-seekers for financial self-sufficiency through job classes and job placement services.
- English Classes provide an on-site space for refugees to learn job-focused English and explore American culture.
- Immigration Legal Services guide former refugees through the legal process on their way to permanent residency or citizenship.

The impact of their work is the result of the hard work of World Relief staff and volunteers, the generosity and prayers of local partners, and the resilience and strength of the refugees and immigrants with whom they work.

To learn more about World Relief or how you can get involved, visit www.worldrelief.org

"Even though World Relief already helped us when we came last February... they still helping us even more. They became our friends. They help us a lot."

- Alan Abdullah

"We went to world relief every morning to learn English for three months and they helped me to get a job. I like World Relief, they are a very good organization for people."

Jeanne D'Ark Musabyimana

"I think of World Relief like part of my family. I can call whenever I want. They are a great family."

- Merhawi Habteab

FIVE WAYS TO HELP REFUGEES

1. **Give**: Your generous giving helps support the efforts of World Relief as they provide services to refugee families in cities across the US. Give a one-time gift or set up a monthly giving plan. You can give directly at worldrelief.org/give.

2. **Volunteer**: There are many ways to work alongside World Relief as a volunteer. You can become a cultural companion, host refugees in your home, assist at a youth program, teach an English class and much more. Visit worldrelief.org/volunteer to learn more about all the opportunities to serve.

3. **Raise Funds**: Even if you do not have a lot of money to give, you likely have a talent or ability that you can use to raise funds. Karisa gives a percentage of the proceeds from every book and painting she sells to World Relief. What can you use to raise funds to support refugees?

4. **Speak Out**: Tell your friends and family that you stand with refugees and encourage them to do the same. We need to have more conversations about supporting refugees in our country. You can use this book as a resource.

5. **Be Kind**: Smile and offer a welcoming handshake to the refugees around you. Be gracious with people who don't speak your language. Be respectful of other cultures. The world can use more kindness towards all people.

FURTHER READING

These resources were particularly helpful for researching information regarding the world refugee crisis. If you are interested in learning more, these sources may be a useful starting point:

WORLD RELIEF
https://worldrelief.org

THE UN REFUGEE AGENCY
https://www.unhcr.org

U.S. COMMITTEE FOR REFUGEES AND IMMIGRANTS
https://refugees.org

REFWORLD
https://www.refworld.org

COUNCIL ON FOREIGN RELATIONS
https://www.cfr.org

HUMAN RIGHTS WATCH
https://www.hrw.org

AMNESTY INTERNATIONAL
https://www.amnesty.org/

ACKNOWLEDGEMENTS

Words cannot express my thankfulness for all the hands that have helped in the love and labor of this book. I am filled with gratitude for the people that have invested in me, in refugees, and this project.

Jordan Marsland, my dear husband, friend and adventure-mate. Thank you for being my place to call home. This book is just as much yours as mine. Thank you for your vision and patience in this adventure, and always stopping to see the view.

Thank you World Relief Seattle. Scott Ellis, Robbie Adams, Liz Nelson, you all were instrumental in making this book happen. Thank you for leading our community in opening our hearts and hands to refugees and asylees, and teaching us that we are better together.

To all my new friends featured in this book, thank you for opening your hearts and homes to us. For stories shared over coffee ceremonies, homemade meals, and picnics. Thank you for teaching me about your beautiful cultures.

Thank you, Natalie Fong Malis, for the hours you spent photographing and editing for this project, offering your advice, vision, and beautiful heart. The majority of the paintings in this book were inspired by Natalie's photography that was instrumental in the level of detail and lighting I was able to achieve in each paint stroke. You can find more of her work at www.nataliefong.com.

Jordan Herman, you are magic the way you so eloquently make sense of my jumbled words. Thank you for late night conversations about Jesus, feminism, and social justice. I wouldn't be who I am today without you.

Thank you David Newcomb for being the first to embark on this adventure with us, and offering your remarkable design expertise to us. Thank you Katie, Joel, and Audrey for letting us borrow him upon occasion.

To all the others who did work on this book. Cathy Joss, Dave Bartlett, the team at the Color Group and everyone at Print Solutions, Inc. Thank you for your masterful work.

To my art instructors and personal mentors, Thank you for not only teaching me art, but showing me what it means to love others in action. Barb Narkaus: For speaking up for me when I believed I had no voice. Mark Terry: For conversations over tea, for India, and endless support. Gary Buhler: For geeking out with me about art and sharing your knowledge. Eric Schutz: For giving us crazy, marginalized high schoolers a safe place to call home.

To all of the friends and family who were so encouraging to me. Thank you for late nights of sharing ideas, labors of love and countless errands. For being our emotional and mental support through this journey. You know who you are and we couldn't have done this without you.

And last but not least, to Jesus, who was a refugee Himself, whose very heart is with the displaced and the marginalized. "We love because He first loved us." John 4:19

Library of Congress Control Number: 2019909254

ISBN 978-1-7331767-5-0

Printed in the United States

FIRST EDITION

**In order to ensure their safety and protect their identities,
certain names and details have been changed.**